The Hound Hut "Book of Dogs"

Colleen Timko & Meranda Hendricks

Copyright © 2012 The Hound Hut
All rights reserved.
ISBN-13:
978-06_5611235 (The Hound Hut Harold)
ISBN-10:
0615611230

ACKNOWLEDGMENTS

The Hound Hut's Colleen Timko and Meranda Hendricks would like to thank their families, friends, and loyal customers who have been there from the very beginning encouraging them every step of the way!

Come on guys just relax!

Just a little tongue tied!

Stealing a kiss

What's behind door #1?

Don't hate me because I'm beautiful!

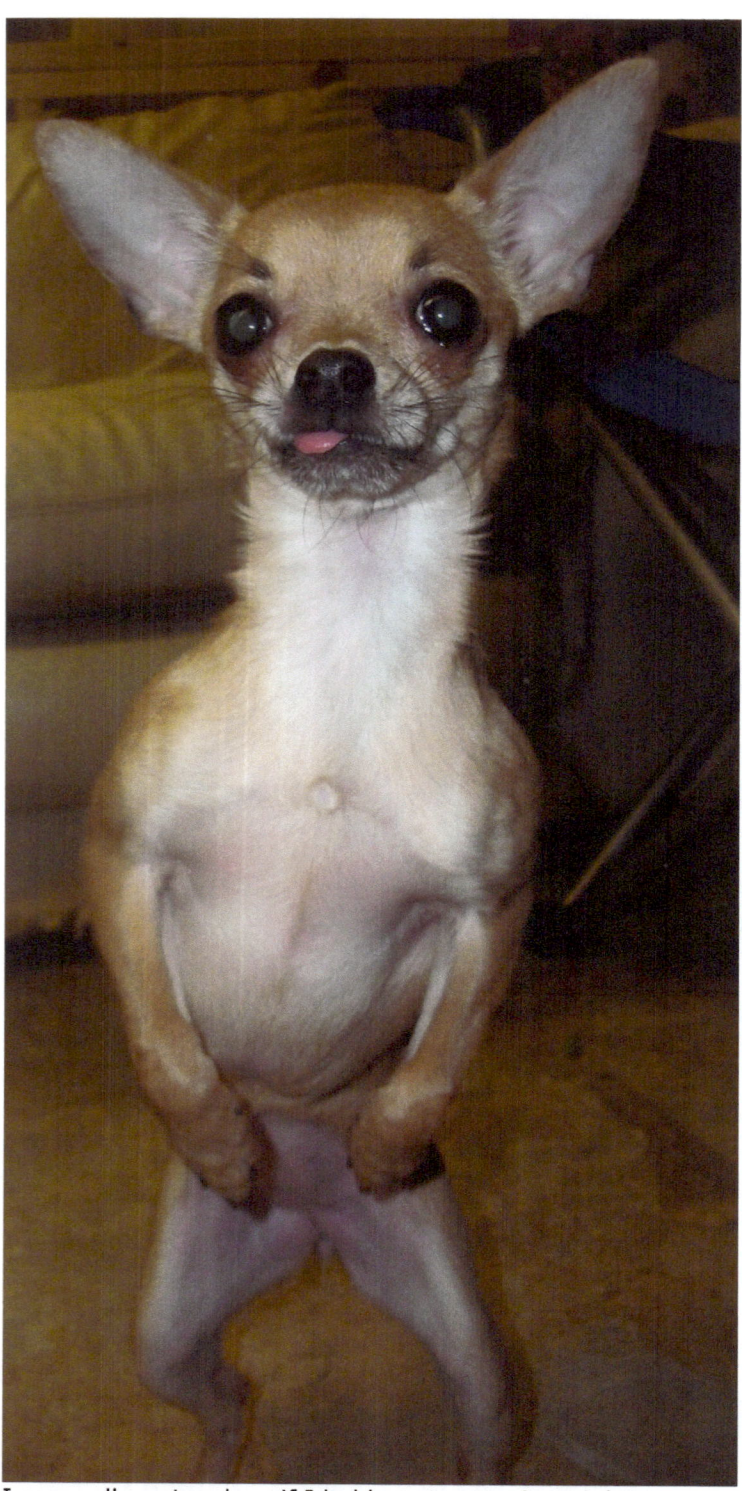
I can walk on two legs if I hold my tongue just right!

I'm ready for my close-up!

Look into my eyes!

Chatting around the water cooler!

Did you say tongues were wagging?

Lip smacking good!

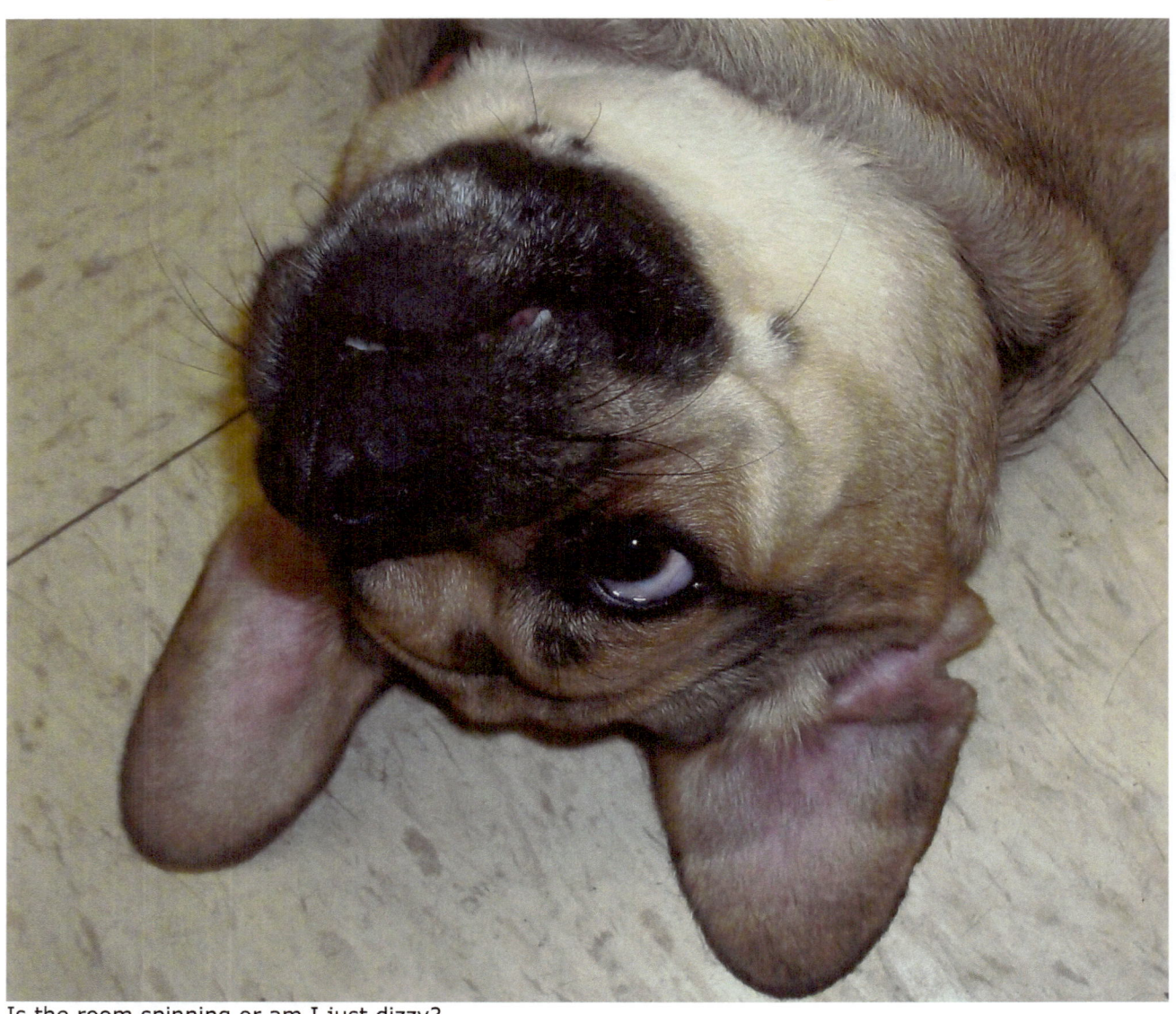
Is the room spinning or am I just dizzy?

Singing the Blues

......and we thank him for our food!

We can always start the diet tomorrow!

Tag! You're it!

May I have a little privacy?

What do you mean bath time?

Word for the day…Breath-Mint!

For me? You shouldn't have!

Not now I'm busy!

Whisper sweet nothings in my ear!

Why doesn't he stay on his side of the chair?

Say ahhhhhhh!

Mr. Sandman bring me a dream!

Please turn off the light!

Party Hound!

Now I lay me down to sleep!

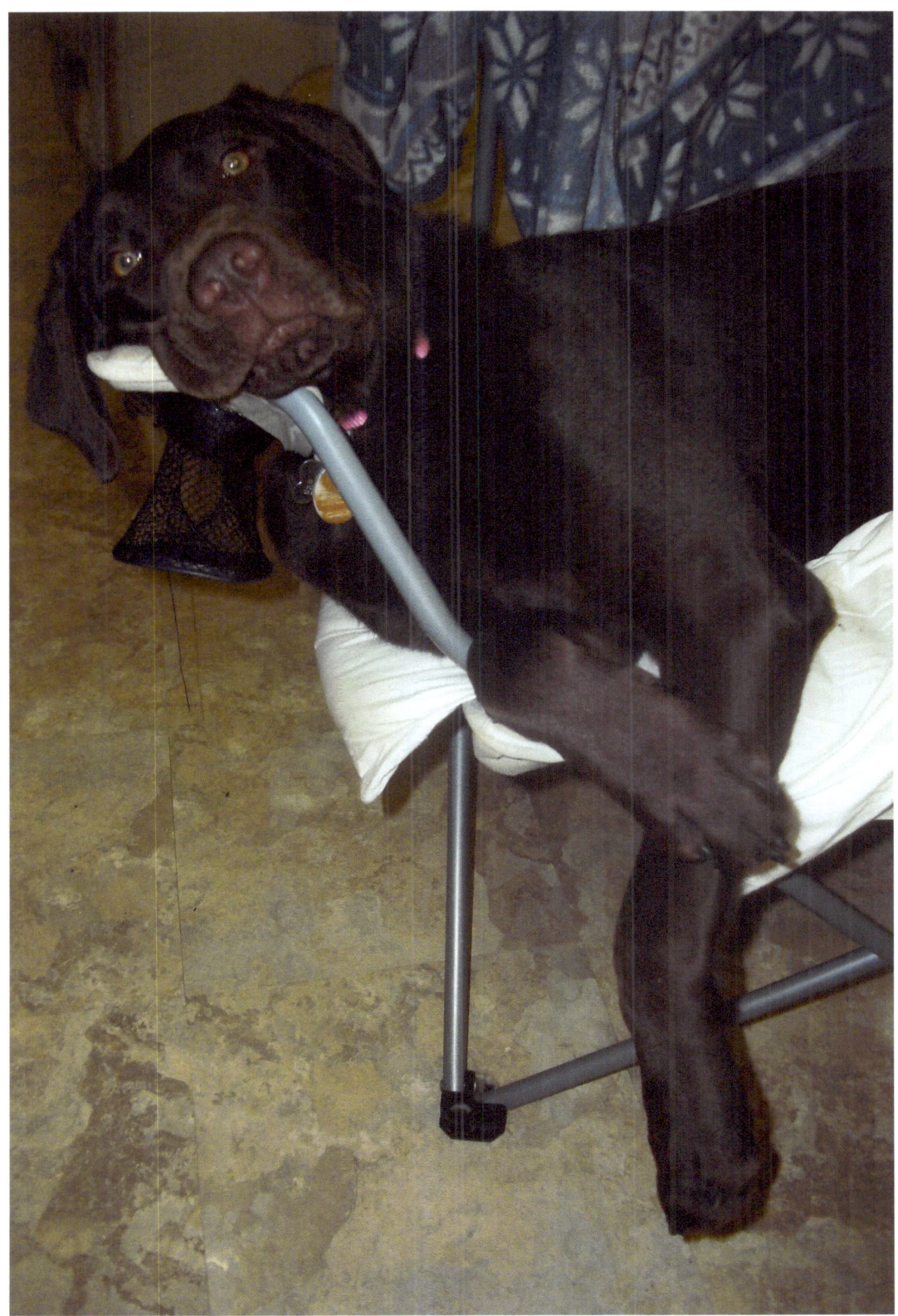

I can't possibly do anything else!

Who did you say was a Q tip?

Where's my stogie?

The latest trend in neckwear!

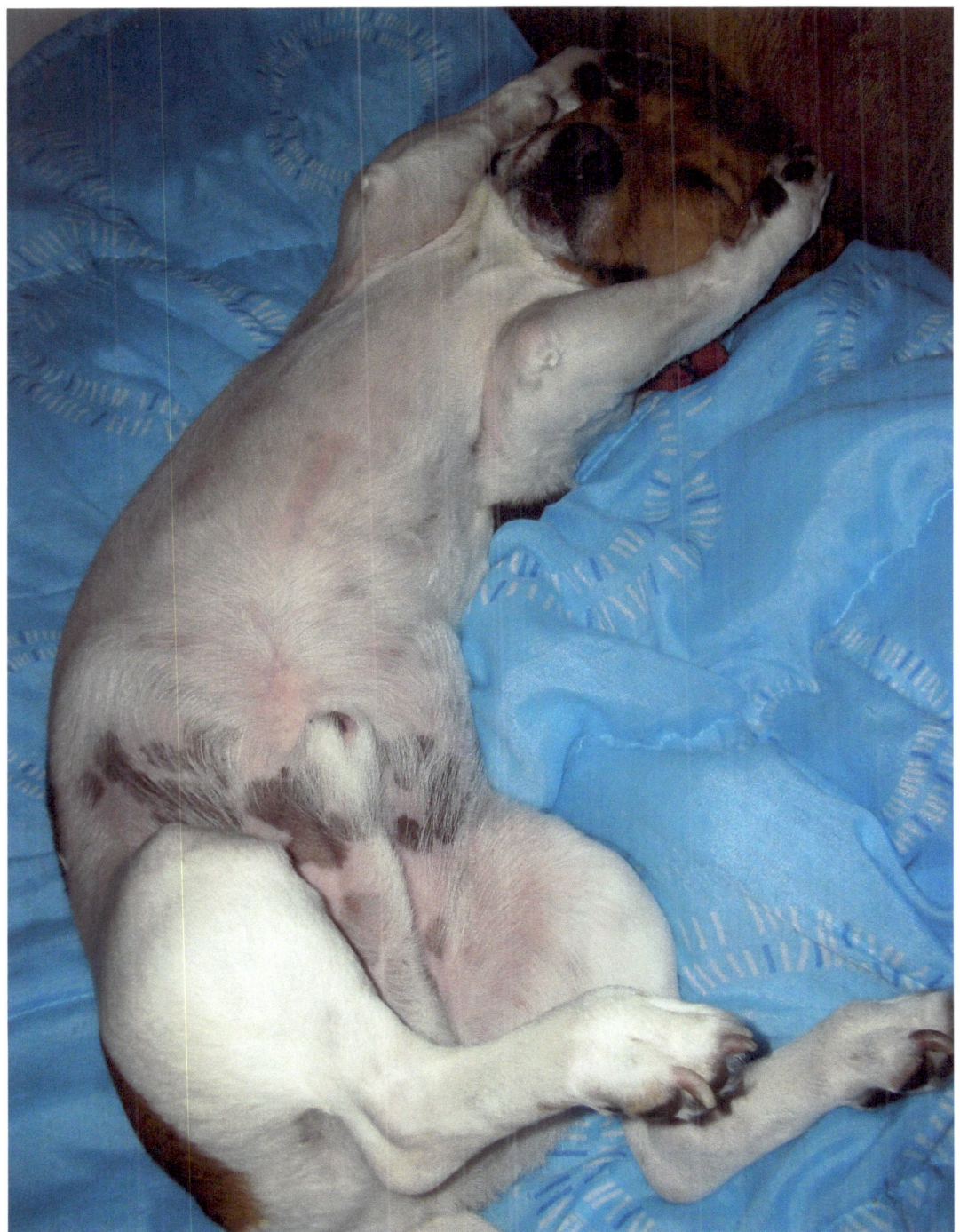

Geez...You need ear plugs around here!

I am gorgeous!

It's a three dog night!

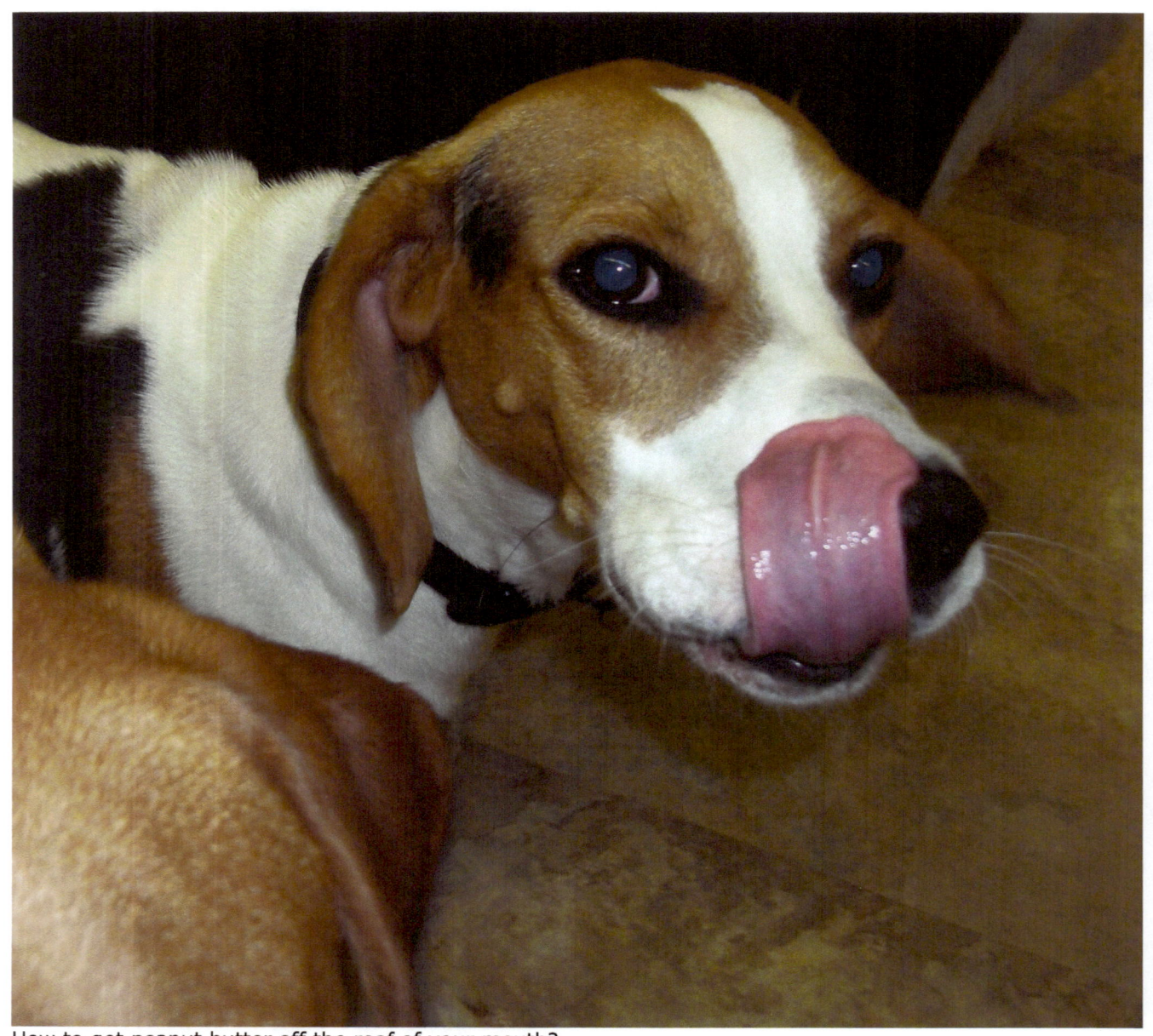
How to get peanut butter off the roof of your mouth?

Sharing is good!

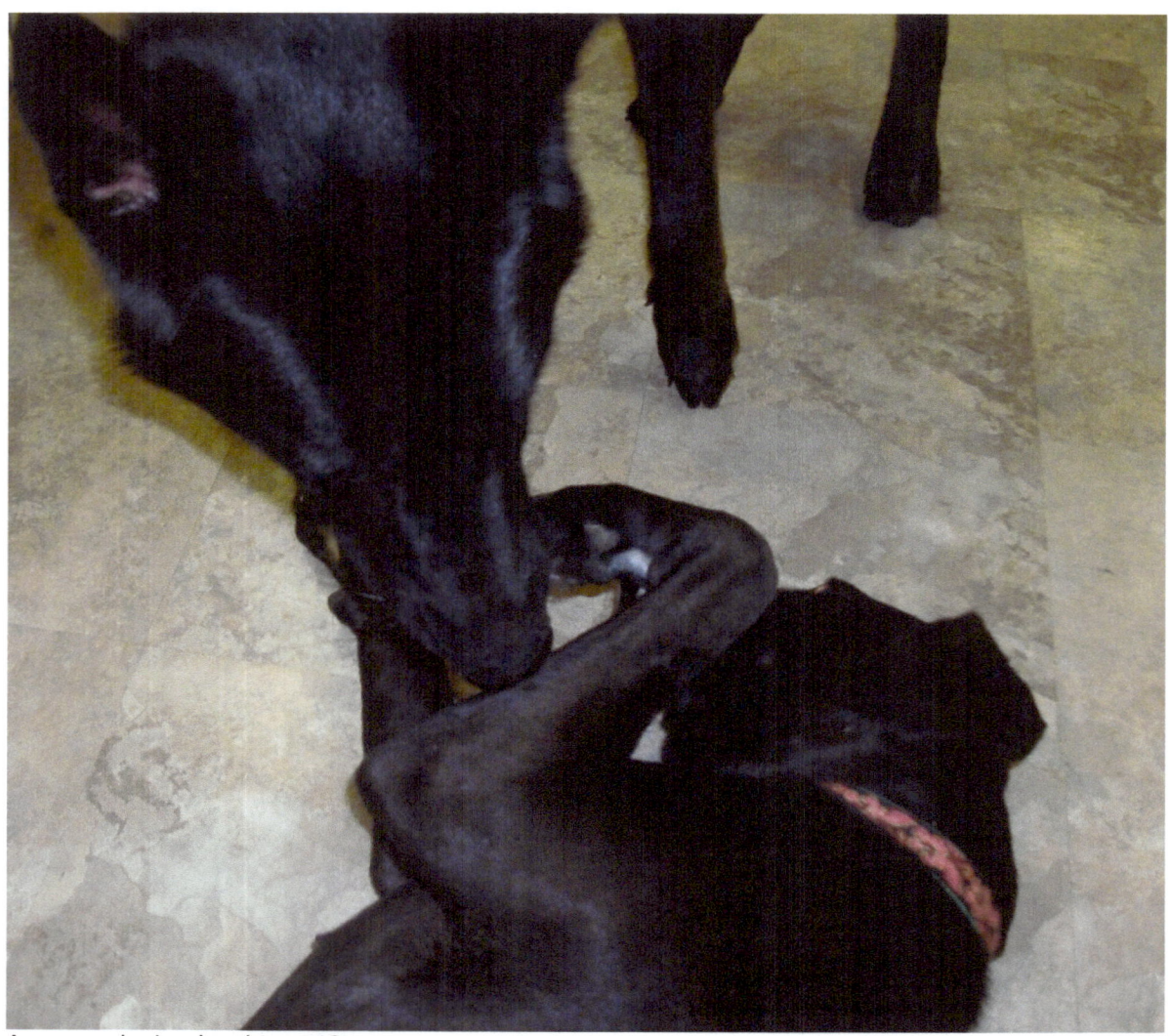
Are you playing hard to get?

No...I said your other left!!

I'm so Hap Hap Happy!

Which way did they go?

Yes I am an angel... Would you like to see my wings?

You crack me up!

There's always one show off in the group!

Number 34 shoots and scores!

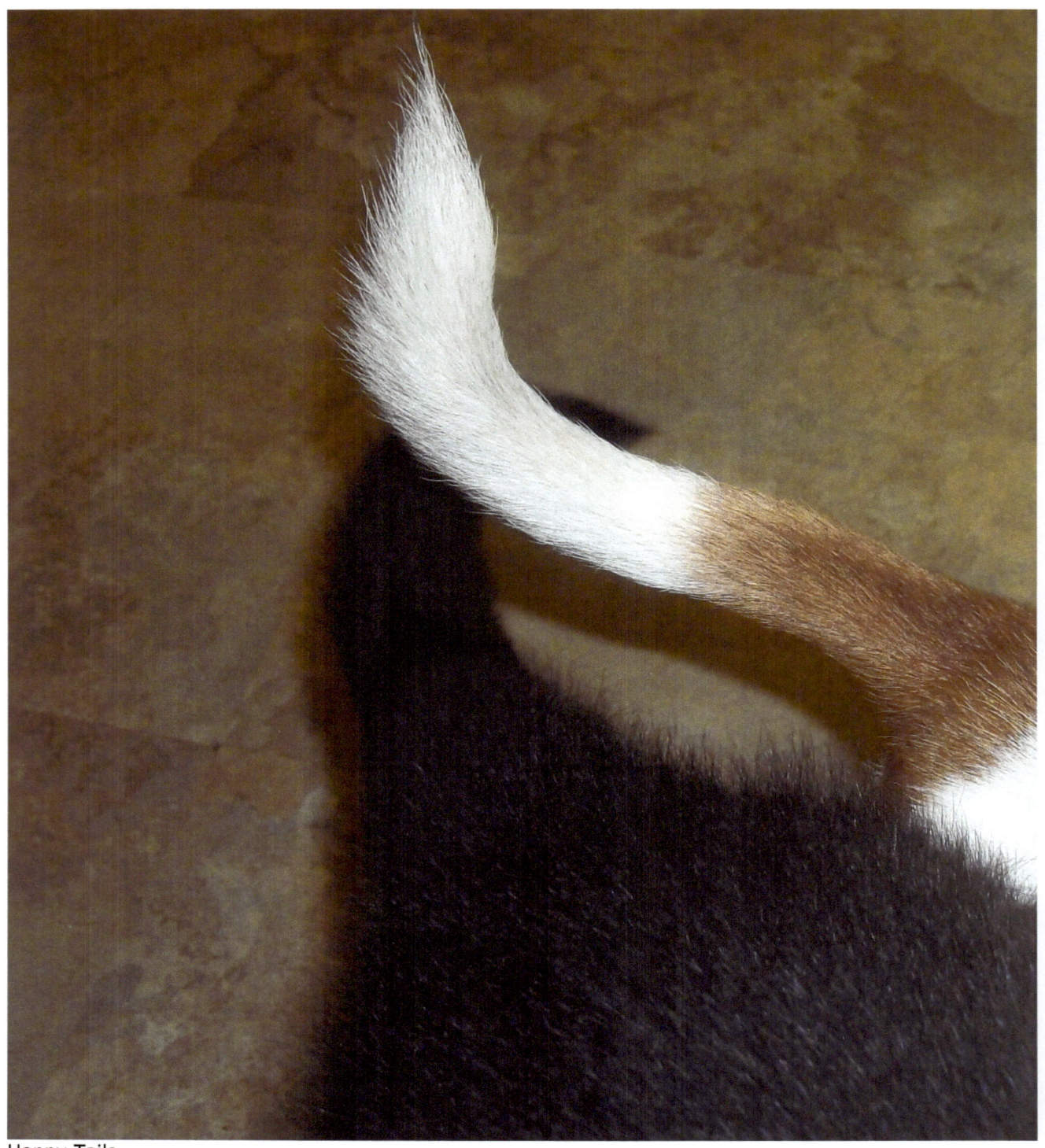
Happy Tails

Making a break for it!

Take me to your leader!

Seriously…..TRICK or TREAT!!

Of course I am an angel!

I'm not sleeping I'm exercising!

Slumber Party!!

Are you the Abominable Snowman?

Dancing doggies!

Just paws for a moment!

I can play anywhere, anytime!

I know I am cute!

Look Mom...no cavities!

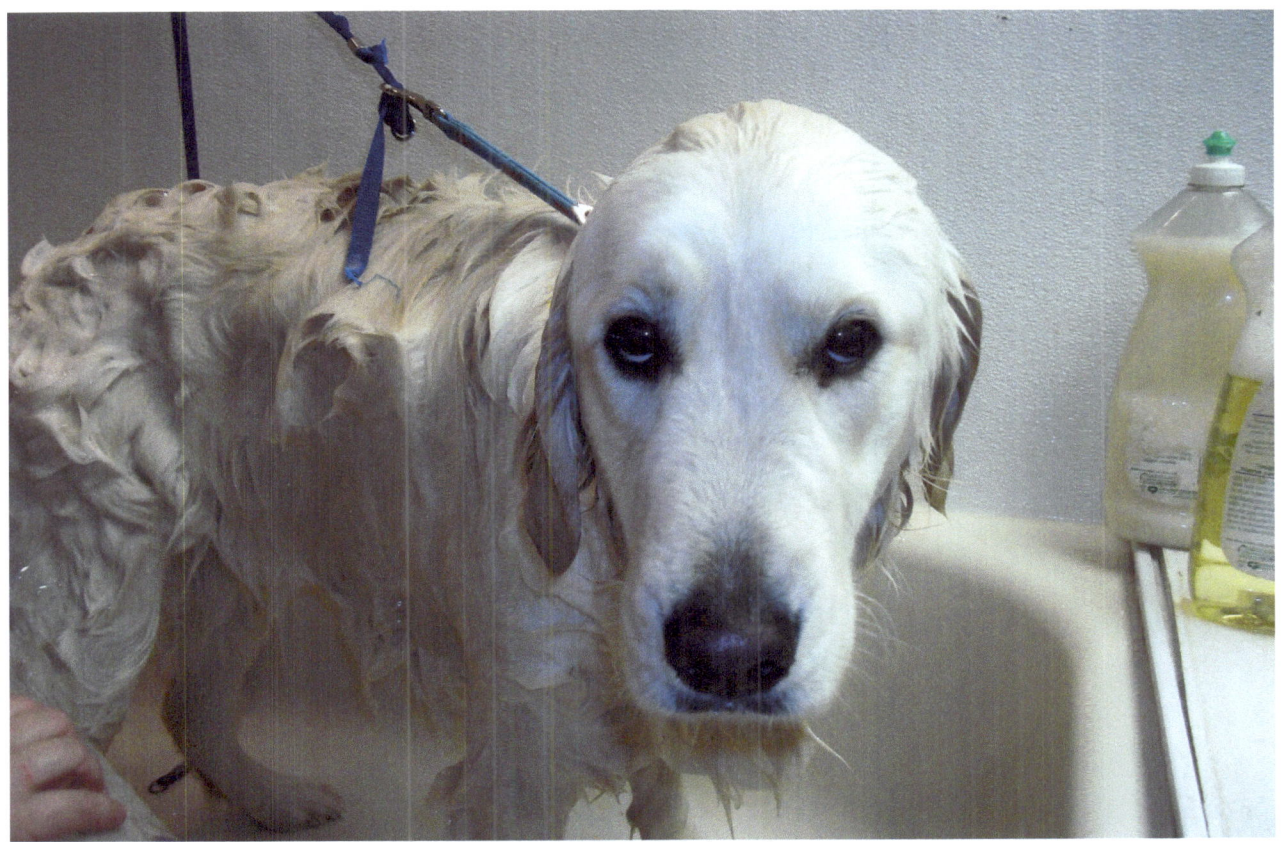

I don't know why every time I swim in the pond I end up here?

Not now.. I'm trying to concentrate!

I've been watching too much television!

This is my best side!

You are getting very sleepy!

Octopus...never leave home without it!

Oh what a big nose you have!

I hear what you're sayin!

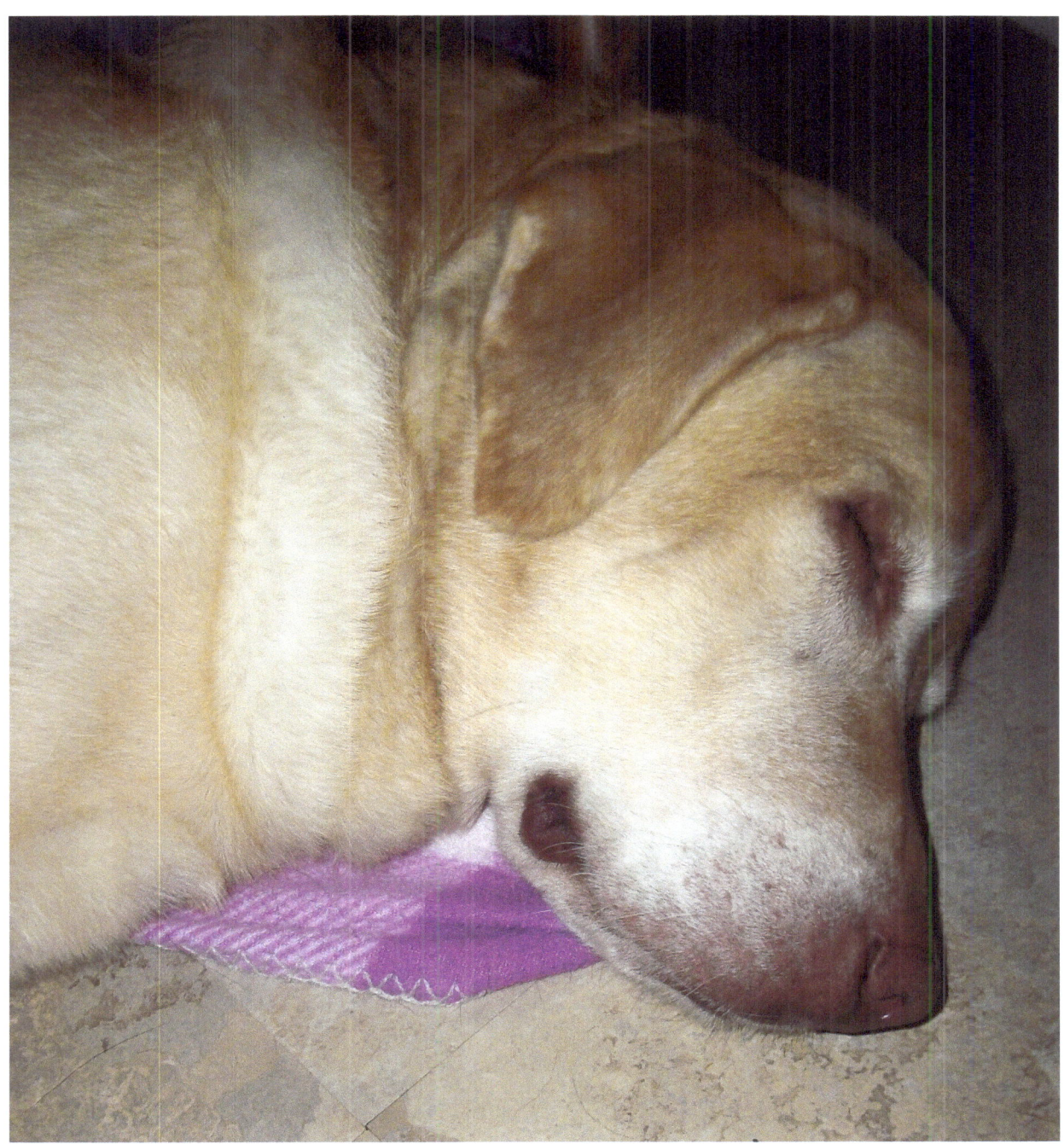
Visions of sugar plums!

Wake up!

Say Cheese!!!

I ain't nothing but a hound dog!

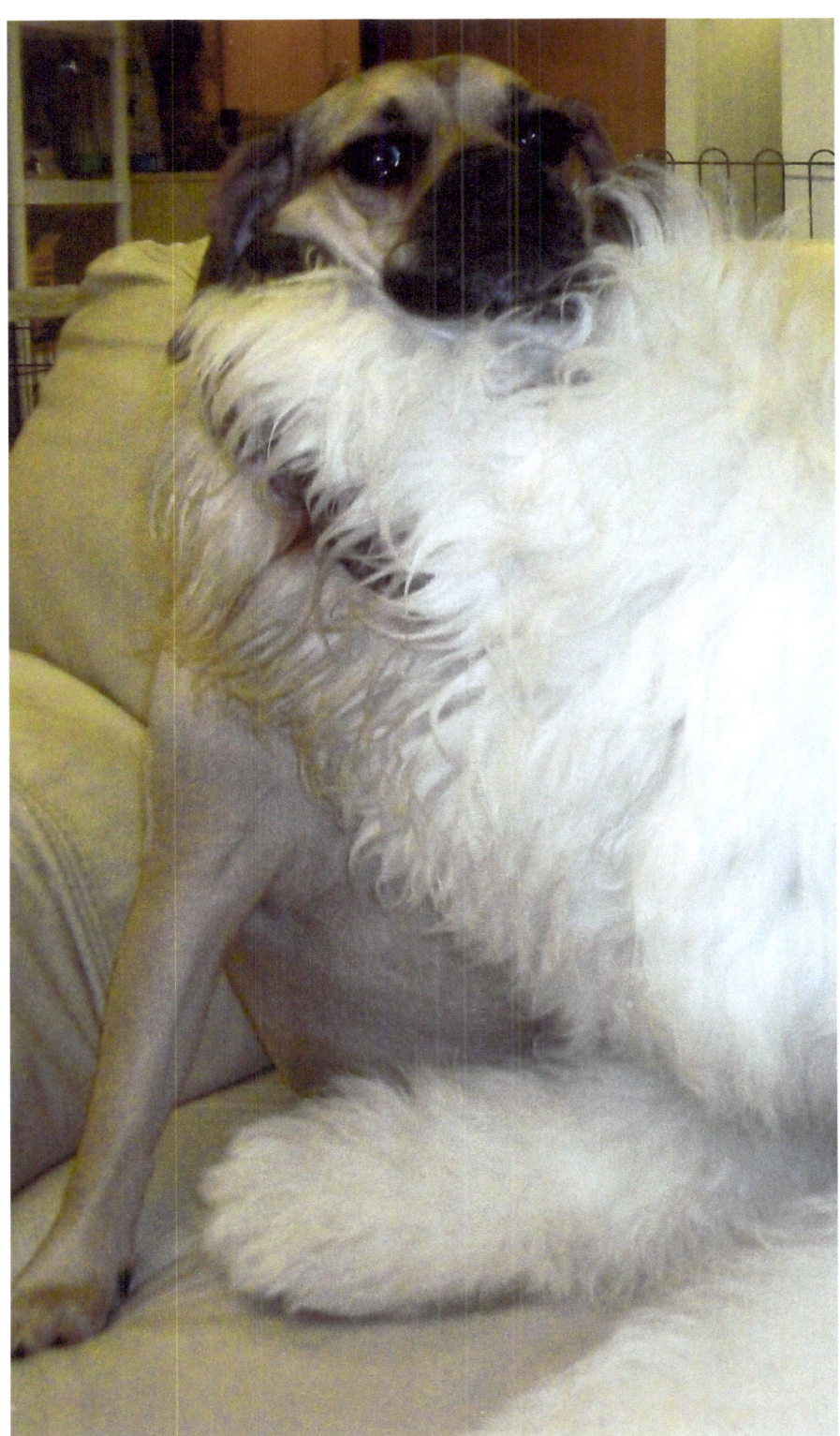

Is that a boa or a sheepdog?

Boo!

Online pet dating?

Where is the popcorn?

Just lean on me!

You want me to do what where?

Did somebody say donuts!

The welcoming committee!

It's a mystery weekend

King of the Jungle!

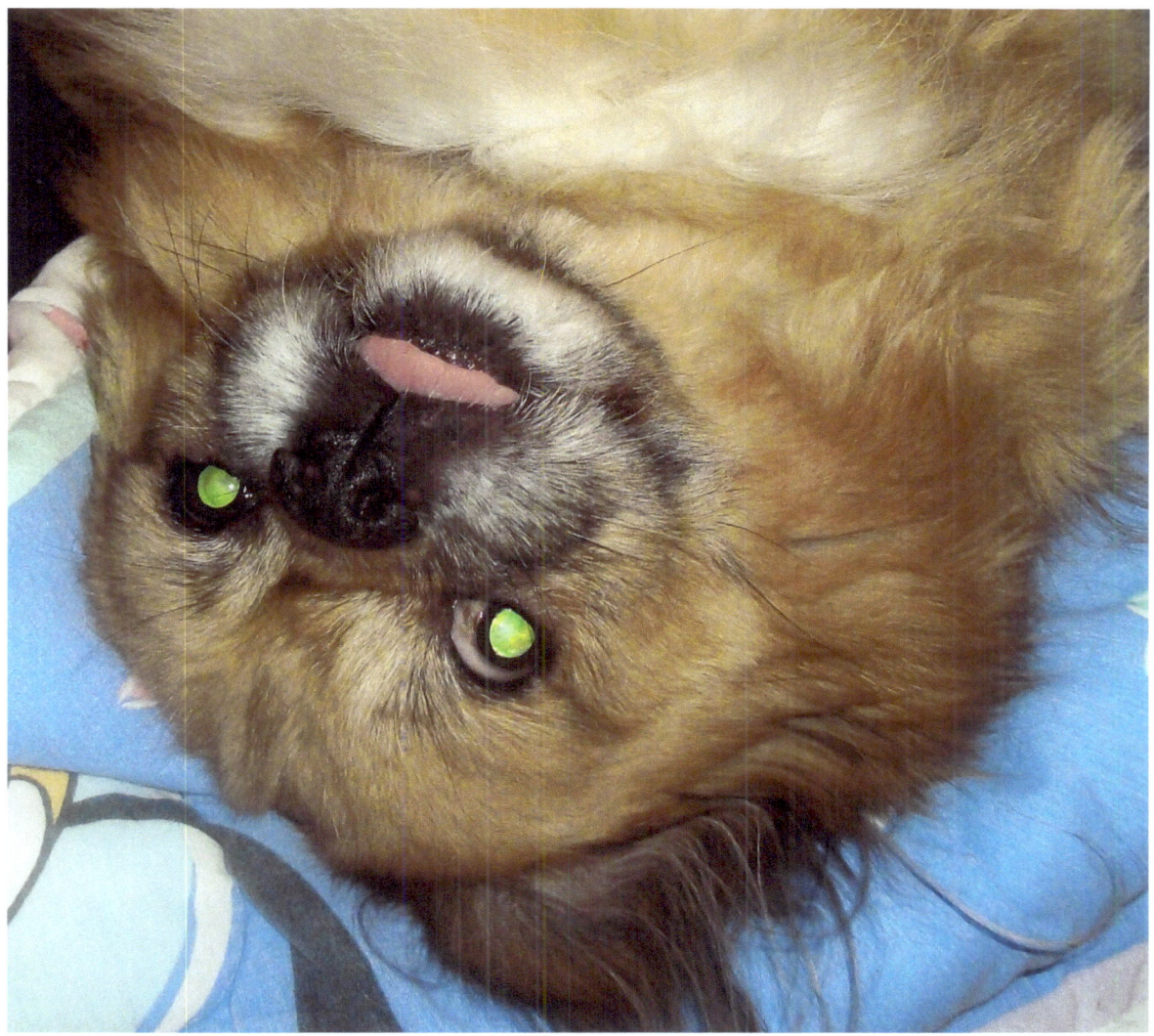
I think I see the big dipper!

I'll look this way and you like that way!

Simon says: Tails up!!

What a night!

Karaoke night!

I've got you babe!

Road Trip!

Did someone say steak?

Wow what a big tail you have!

Rise and Shine

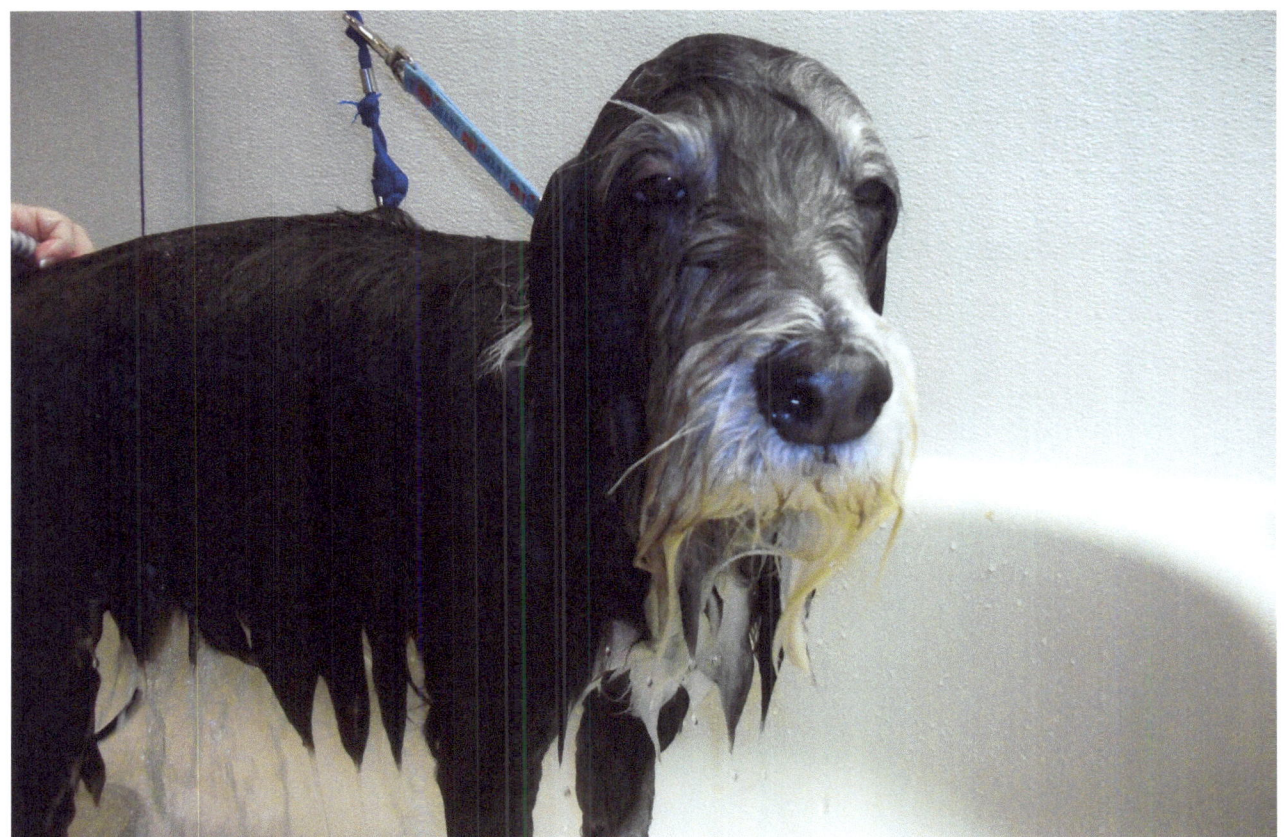
I'm so running through the mud puddle when I am out of here!

Oh my what big teeth you have!

I was dreaming of burritos!

Now that I got your attention!

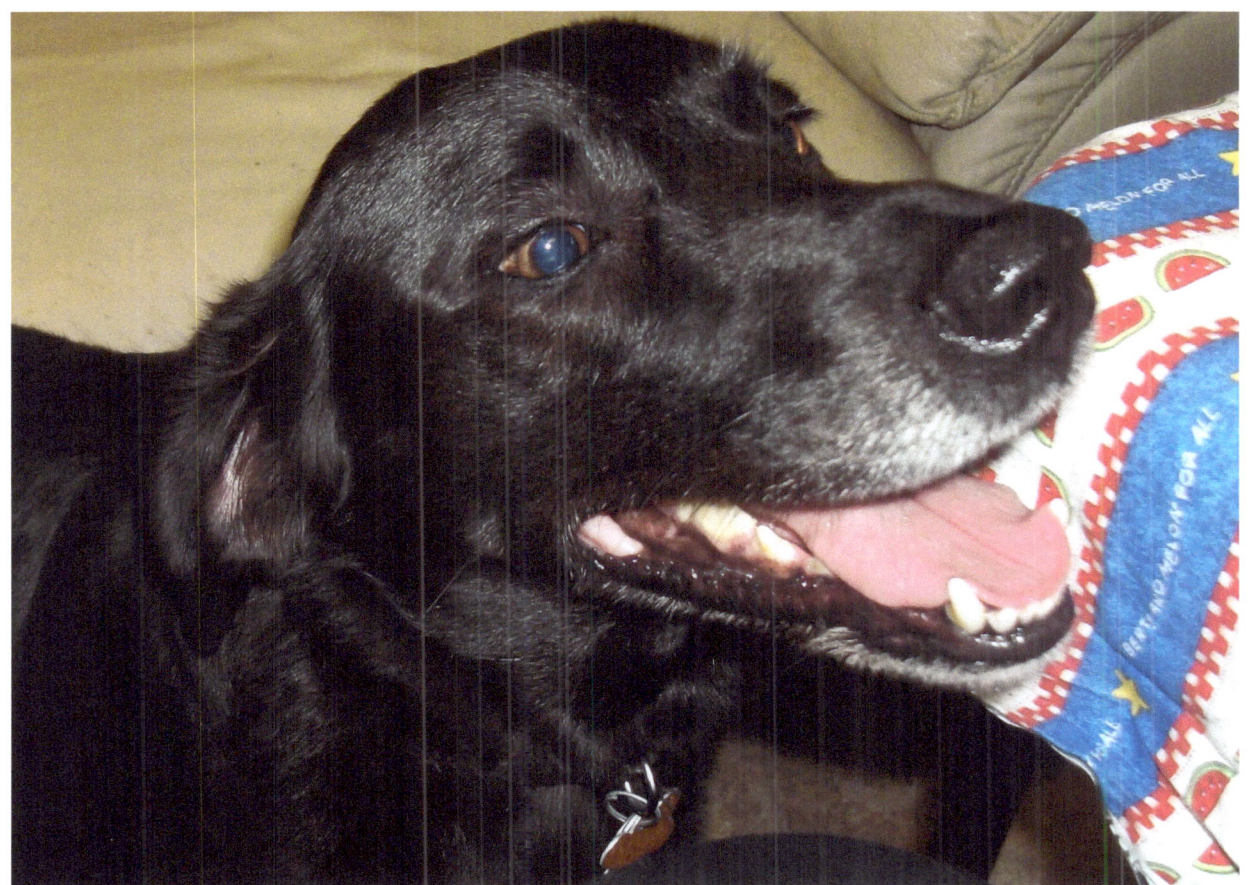

Got Treats?

Black Tie Event?

I've got your back!

Catching a ride

My teeth are bigger than yours!

Can you hear me now?

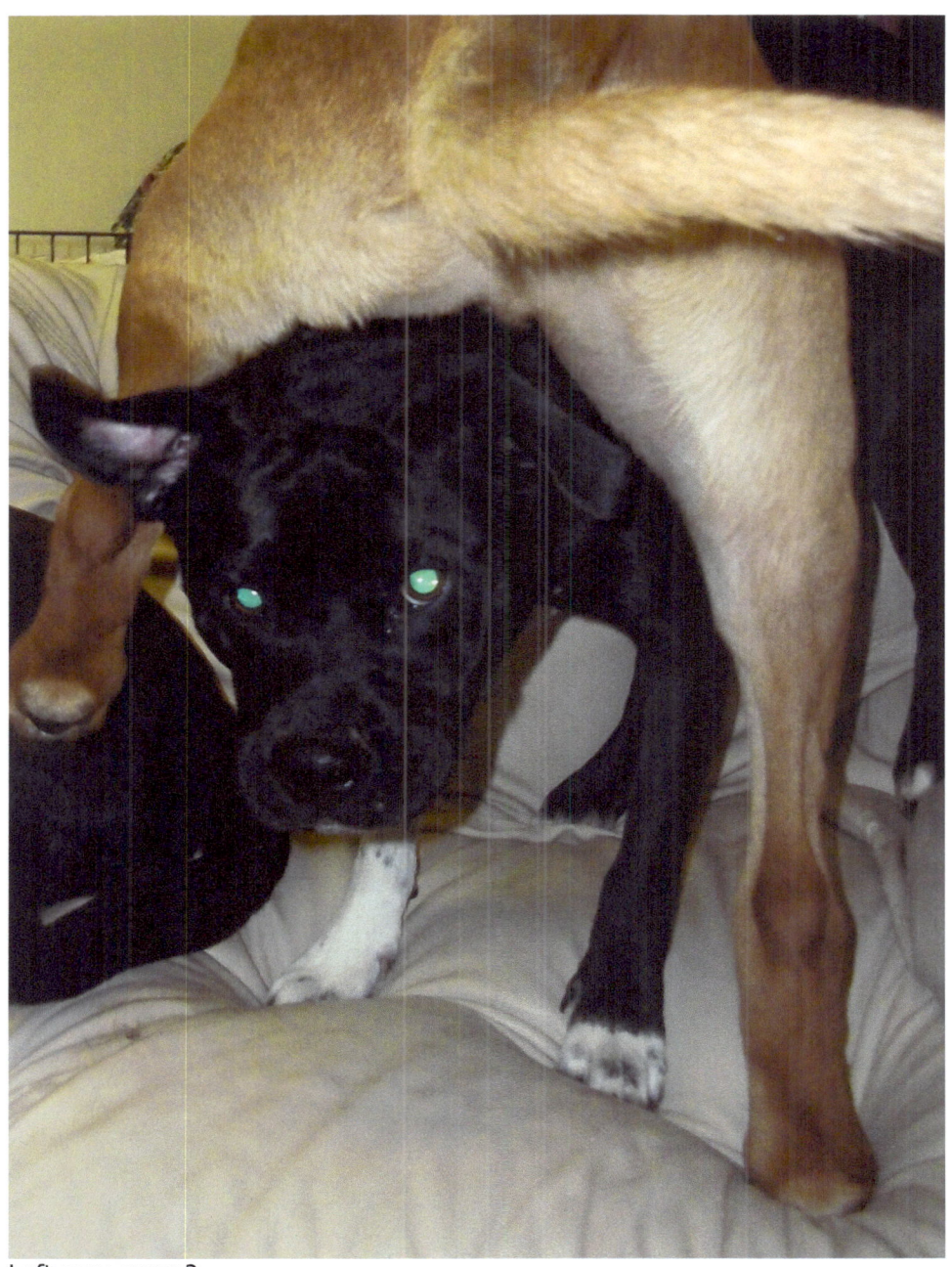

Left paw green?

Ready for take off!

Its just one of those days when you want to pull the covers up over your head!

Have you met my hedgehog?

Ladies Man!

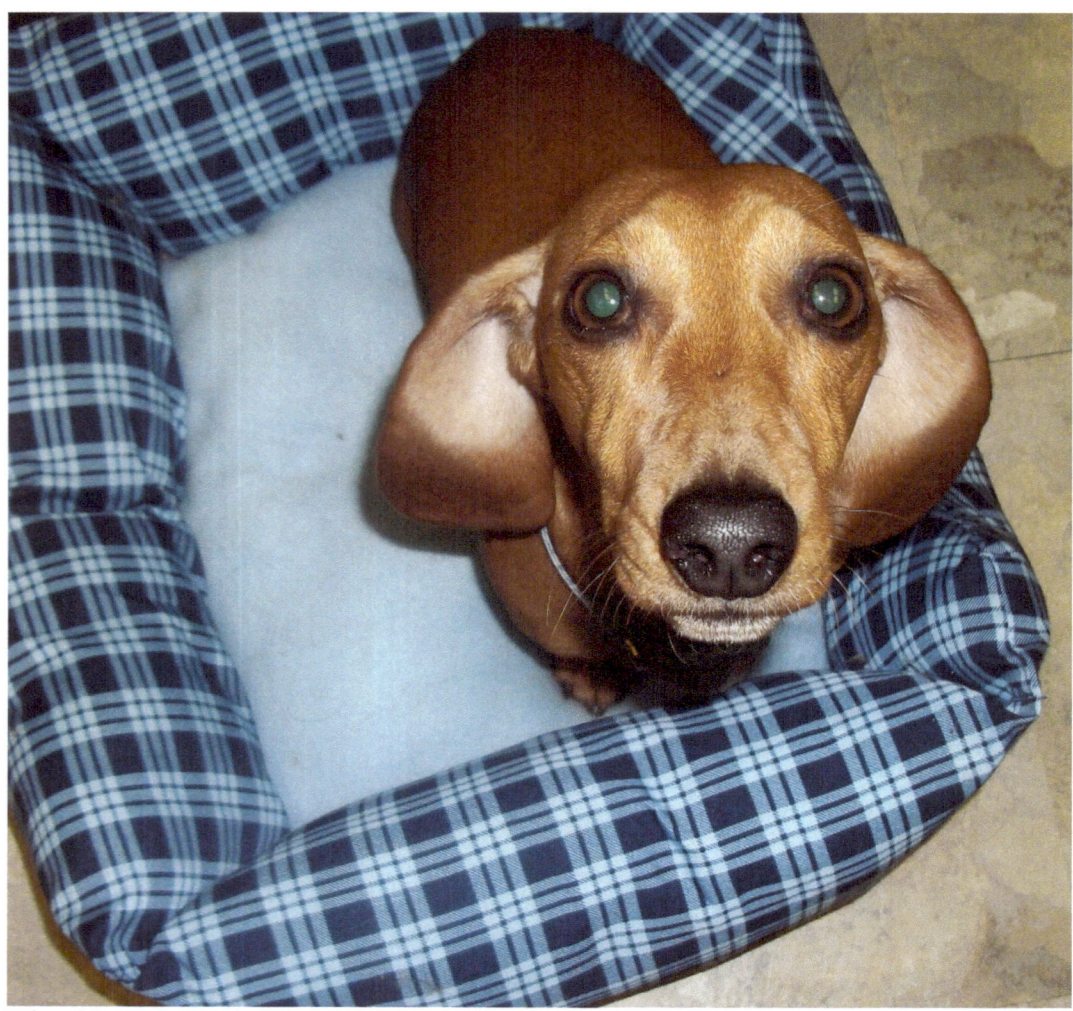

What big ears you have!

One, Two...Cha Cha Cha

She is a little scary!

Nothing like a clean toy!

Open wide

A diva....who? me?

Is that your ride?

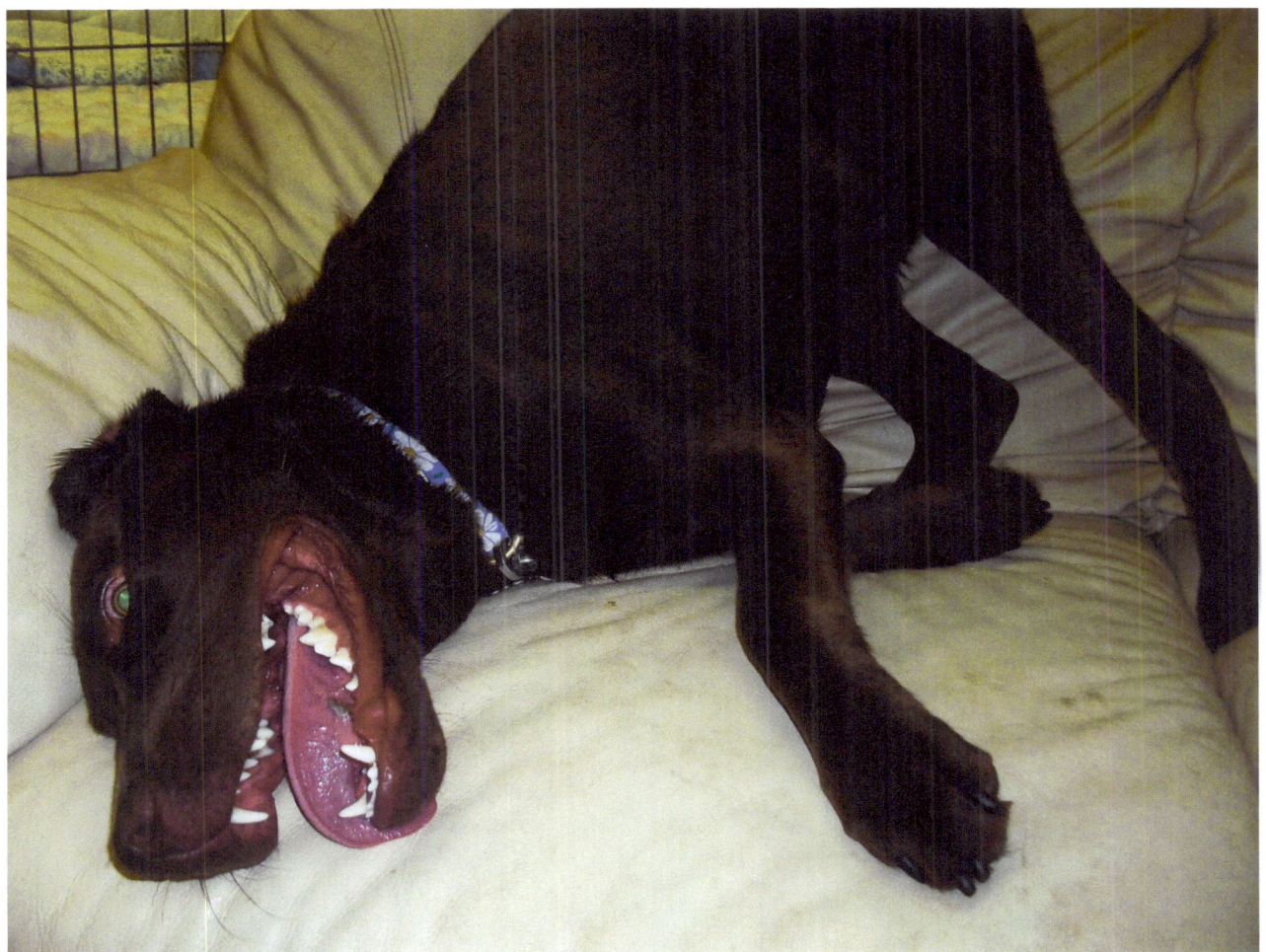
Can't stop....must keep playing.

Excuse me... I think you have my tongue

Look mom no batteries!

The chicken sandwich looks good!

Catch me if you can!

If you want a groom......get in line!

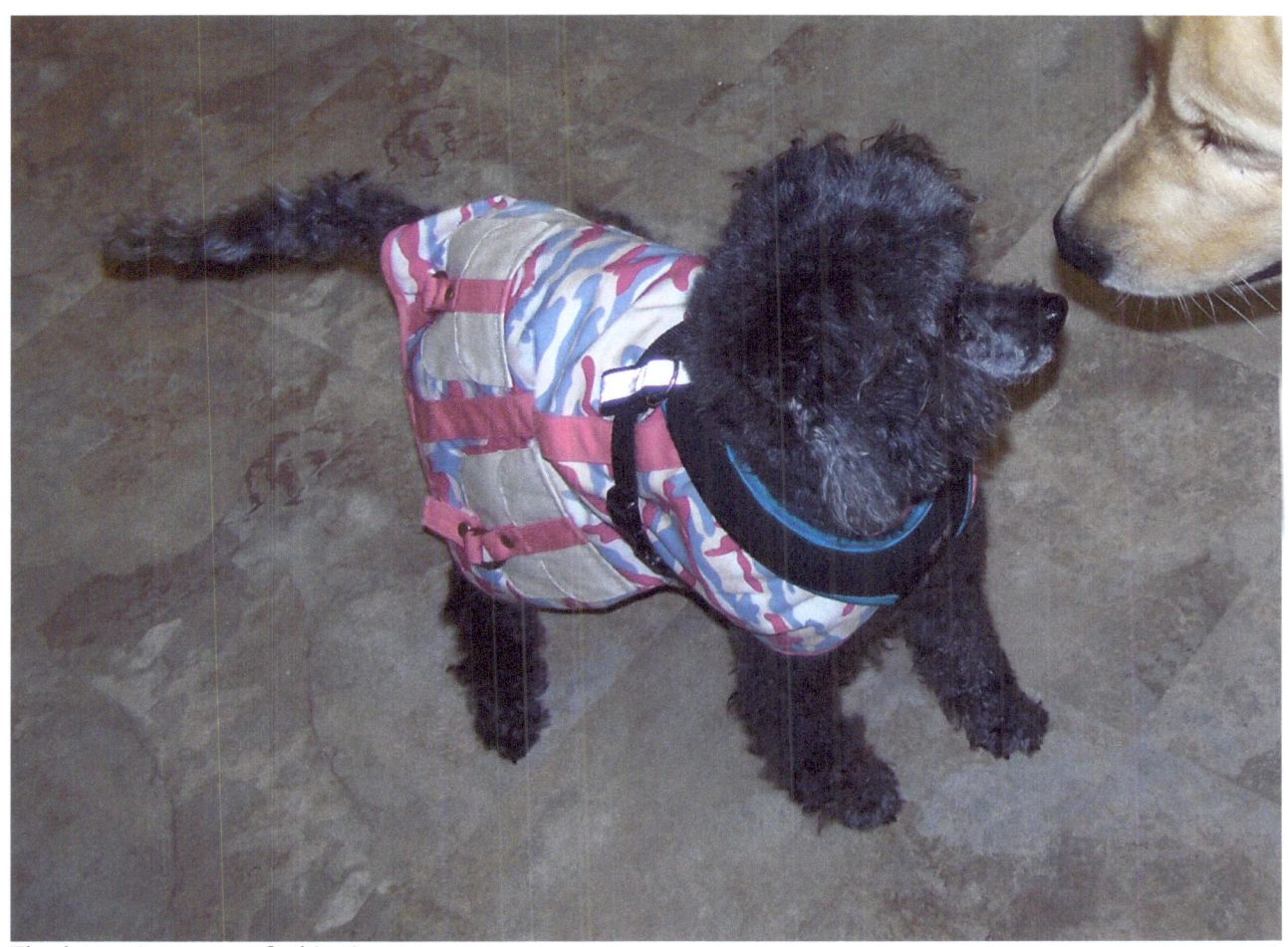
The latest in runway fashion!

Snug as a bug in a rug!

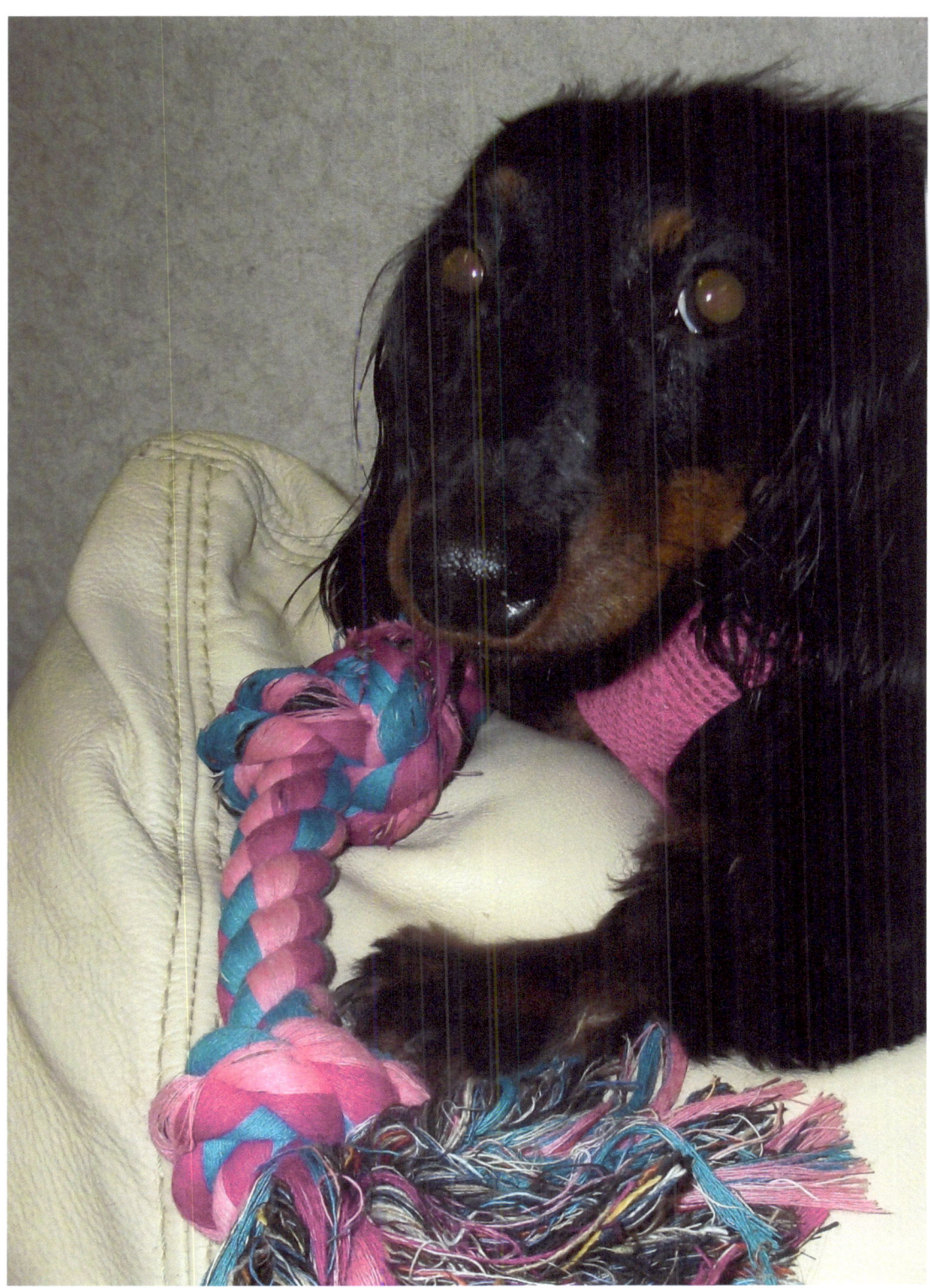

No paws about it...purple is my favorite color!

You are supposed to grab the other end

Sweet Dreams

See ya again soon!

ABOUT THE AUTHORS

Colleen Timko and her friend Meranda Hendricks often talked about opening their own doggie daycare. When chatting about their own dogs they began the dialog on what they envisioned would be the perfect dog daycare. Happy dogs that go home wanting to come back was just one of the criteria. Treating each dog special making their experience a happy one was the main goal.

In November 2008 Colleen's husband Marty called home frantic from work informing her that his department had just been downsized. He and his coworkers were immediately terminated.

The Timko's muddled though the holidays and in January 2009 Colleen was informed that the division in which she worked would be sold and she would also lose her job. It was time for Colleen to think seriously about the future.

With the urging and support of her husband, Colleen called Meranda and they met to talk about starting a dog daycare. Meranda was very excited even though she knew that with the economic downturn it would not be easy. Still they were both enthusiastic and ready to get started.

Two years later The Hound Hut located in Gahanna Ohio, a suburb of Columbus is growing every day. Colleen began photographing the dogs originally for enjoyment and to post them on The Hound Hut's website and social networking site for families to check in for updates. Since then it has become a popular daily check in for those wanting to catch the latest antics!

Colleen and Meranda wanted to create this photo book of dogs with captions to bring a smile and maybe even a laugh to others. When feeling the stress of the day, just think of the dogs at the Hound Hut and you can't help but smile!

www.houndhutcolumbus.com

www.ingramcontent.com/pod-product-compliance
Lightning Source LLC
Chambersburg PA
CBHW041958150426
43194CB00002B/52